Dandelion Seed

Cait Warner

BookLeaf Publishing

Presentation by *BookLeaf Publishing*

Web: www.bookleafpub.com

E-mail: info@bookleafpub.com

ISBN: 9789395950497

First edition 2023

DEDICATION

For Gran, Flower fairies and rooibos tea, you were the essence of love.

You still inspire me every day.

For Adam T., You made a new world less scary, you were a light in a dark place.

You are still so loved.

PREFACE

"I am a wayfarer, a dandelion seed that people catch for a second, fill me with their hopes, dreams and wishes, then they throw me away to the wind."

Aware

Aware.

I am so intensely aware of how everything is a beautiful and tragic process of growing and fading; how the poppies in my mother's garden, blooming only yesterday, have their petals laying now decaying in the soil below their empty centers.

How one day my mother will no longer be here to tend her garden, how this landscape will change, how I will have changed.

I am so aware that each person I meet, will grow with me and we will wilt eventually, together or apart; how eventually there will only be memories.

How eventually there will be no one to remember.

I am so intensely aware.

Picture Frames

Faded pictures stand in silver picture frames,
displaying a world that no longer exists,
a young girl, a young boy.

We stood small,
on the edge of cracked stone,
far away from home,
but together, together was home.

Faded pictures sting,
holding memories that we can never return to,
a family.

We have grown,
we still stand small,
we are stuck in the memory of stone,
both now farther away from home,
no longer together, we are lost.

Home only lives on in silver picture frames.

Not Here

The world is suddenly still and darkened,
it is grey, suspended in a moment between
ignorance and pain.

There is not a breath of wind,
no light to undulate softly through the window
pane,
no song from the birds, or beat from your heart.
You are not here.

I close my eyes.

I am not here.

No, the leaves will not fall,
the sky will not change,
the moon will not rise and nor the sun,
for I cannot rise without you.

I am not here.

I open my eyes.

You are not here, you are gone.

Flower

I tried to see myself as a flower, I tried to blossom...

I realize now that means I am relying on the rain and the sun,
or someone like you to water me and keep me warm.

I am relying on the unreliable and you don't care for flowers.

I don't want to be a flower.

Sometimes

Sometimes I think I feel you in the breeze on the
eve of a new moon, or hear you in the tapping
on my window on a rainy night.

It makes me feel more alone.

Sometimes I dream of you, I never see you,
you're only in the shadows in the backgrounds,
behind the trees, or the clouds, buildings or open
doors, always just out of reach.

I don't think you are real anymore.

Sometimes I close my eyes and wish for a
distant shore where I feel nothing in the breeze
but the warmth from a sunset that waves to me
as it settles into the reflections of the ocean, I
hear nothing but the whispering of the sea as it
ebbs onto the sand, reminding me the world is
still beautiful even if I am experiencing it on my
own.

I still ache in secret.

Front Door

I can still smell the scent of the roses outside
your front door,
the grass and the pebbles, I can still hear the
rustle of the leaves in the trees that overhang the
path that leads to your front door.

I can still see the white picket fence and the gate,
the road and the sidewalk that guides me to your
front door.

I see the park across the street, I see the houses
that surround yours, the blue skies and the sun
that shines on the roof that sheltered you, it was
yours.

I see the windows with curtains open, letting the
light in,
I hear the distant laughter reverberate from
inside, I feel your warmth.

I hear the echo of my knock on your front door.
You answer in my memory, but no one is home
anymore.

Reminded

I was wrapped in his fantasy,
like a comforting story or a warm cup of tea.

I forgot that they all end eventually.

He is not a bedtime story or even a cup of tea,
all he did was leave me cold and empty.

I was reminded how all things come and go as
quickly as they arrive.

We are perpetually left with spaces to be filled
by the new, as they ache for the old.

Longing

I long for feelings that I have lost to the past.

I yearn for people who no longer exist,
for the connections that were severed by time,
distance and change.

They appear to me like figures barely visible in
heavy mist,
I feel them in songs, smells and sceneries.

Maybe these are the only places I will ever find
them now.

Wonder

Sometimes I wonder how many missed
encounters I have passed by each day;

How many people I might have known,
How they might have changed my life,
How they all could have led to anywhere but
here,
to anyone but you.

Sand

You are, you always were, here in my hands,
slipping like the sand from the beach where I
wept out every last memory of you and me.

You, taking each molecule of my soul away,
from this shell that encases my very being,
leaving me restless and shattered, needing you to
make me whole again.

Why can't I ever keep you?

Sand Dunes

For months I have been with you, eyes closed at
the sand dunes;

Encased in our bubble, listening to the waves
and the seagulls.

For months I have been dreaming of warmth, of
sun and early morning skies.

For months I have been holding onto the
stability of your hand;

Ignoring the world outside as it crumbles around
me.

For months I have been replaying every moment
I wish I could return to, wondering if I'll ever
wake up.

If only I knew.

For months I have been with you, eyes closed
safe at the sand dunes;
Encased in our bubble, nothing beyond us,
nothing behind us.

For months I have been hiding within this moment.

If I could go back...

If only I listened to my soul as it shivered in the cold as I drove home;

If only I followed it back to the sand dunes, the warmth, the sun, morning skies and you.

For months I have been trying to find my way home;

Fearing the future, begging for the past,

For months I have been hoping you'd still be there.

I am here now, eyes open, alone at the sand dunes; I ran out of time.

If only I knew.

I am.

I am a stone,

Engraved with the epitaphs of every self I have ever been.

I am a branch,

Cut from my childhood, my roots, my leaves.

I am crumbling,

With every etching those who come and go leave on me.

I am wilting,

Every new root severed, each new leaf taken from me.

How do I rebuild who I was?

How do I grow?

I can't remember who I am.

Comfort

I find more comfort from the floor than I do in
my bed, I should feel safe in my sheets, my
blankets and pillows...

But I find monsters and memories under the
covers, they brush my skin as I try to dream,
they whisper his words in my ear.

I feel safer sleeping alone.

Corners

Here's to the corners of small rooms,
Where the floor feels safer,
and the world feels more secure.

Birds

Against grey skies, their shadows weave through powerlines and trees; For years I have wondered where they are going, and I have yearned to go with them.

I hope they pass you by and tell you how I still think of you whenever I am alone.

Evergreen

Bending at the tops of trees
are the last of the fragile summer leaves,
as though they still hope to be evergreen;
It’s the saddest thing I've ever seen.

Today I sat with my sadness

Today I sat with my sadness.

I looked into its eyes and saw my soul staring
back at me; It held me in its arms and I gave
way to its embrace.

Today I sat with my sadness.

Tired of fighting, we sit here in silence, at peace.

A Love Letter To My Past

You are all the opportunities that were never
realised.
Everything that could have been, but wasn't.

I have always been unable to stop myself from
looking back, into the sunset and through the
horizon into everything that once was,
everything that no longer is.

I see it all replay, I watch helpless and feel the
pull of emotions that live on in that distance, I
stand on the precipice of an ocean that's tide
only leads to you, to the past.

Sometimes a piece of my soul gets caught in this
tide and is lost to me.
As it swirls around in reveries and summer
evenings that I can no longer touch; I feel it
calling to the rest of me, an echo of home, of
comfort.

You look so much warmer out there past the
horizon, and it is so cold here, in between you
and the future.

I hear it calling to me from time to time, urging me to leave you and let you fade out into inky black, to let the ocean take itself away from the edge where I stand, to let my soul replace itself in new ways.

It asks me to turn my face to its sunrise, it tells me there's more to see, but I have to look away from you if I want to experience it all.

I'm at the in-between, I need to breathe out and let your ocean take my fears to you, and away from me.

Must I go alone?

Take my fears.
Take my pain.
Take the sunsets and release me to the new sunrise.

Needing Change

I can feel the seasons changing,
I need to migrate with the birds,
I can feel the moon pulling,
I need to move with the tide.

The wind has changed its course
and I am a dandelion seed who must change
course with it.

Milton Keynes UK
Ingram Content Group UK Ltd.
UKHW022007011223
433620UK00014B/729

9 789395 950497